AF447676

ild have

ist a dre

.

.r Allan

ascinat

I can st

of dar

foe

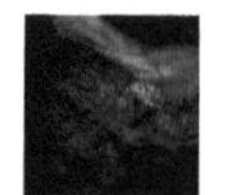

....

....

red of 1

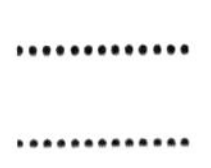

y

orns

oor

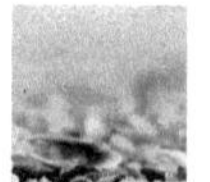

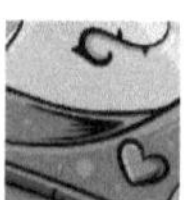

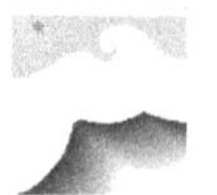

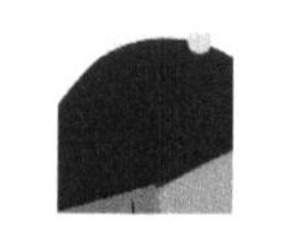

ıal

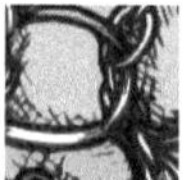

ieces o

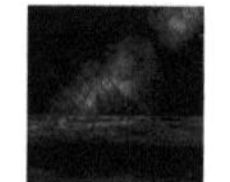

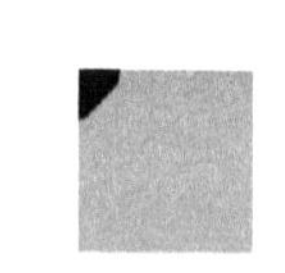

ess,

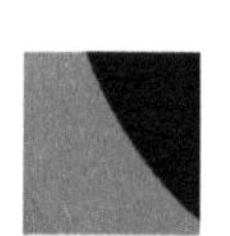

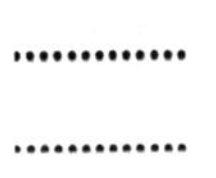

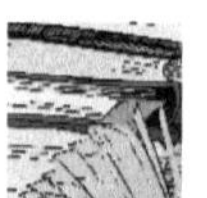

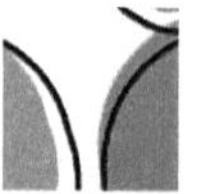

mistake

t your n
n

y

t I am,

 you

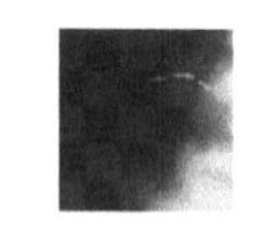

of love a

ving

on you

ng,

soul

ory

m?

ιe lies, a

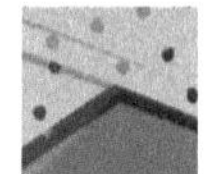

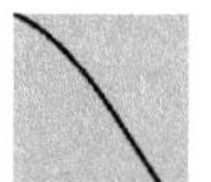

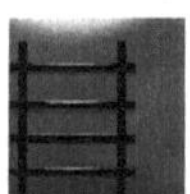

Appdx

ersweet

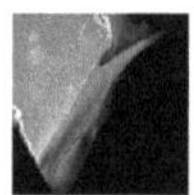

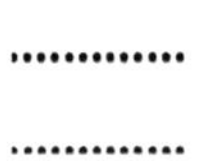

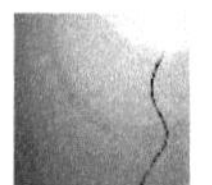

ıd foun

under
l run?

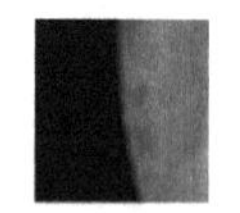

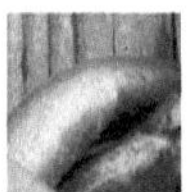

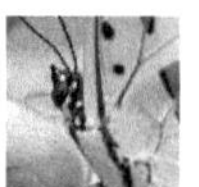

ions

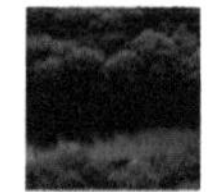

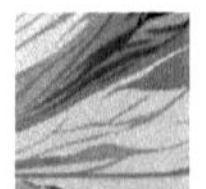

and

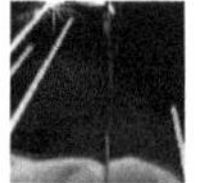

in

notions

rs

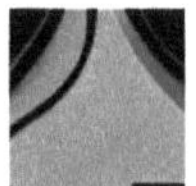